Especially for

_____

From

_____

Date

_____

Happiness Is...

A Shared Smile

(AND OTHER SECRETS BETWEEN FRIENDS)

BARBOUR
PUBLISHING

Published by Barbour Publishing, Inc., P.O. Box 719, Uhrichsville, Ohio 44683, www.barbourbooks.com

Our mission is to publish and distribute inspirational products offering exceptional value and biblical encouragement to the masses.

 Member of the
Evangelical Christian
Publishers Association

Printed in China.

Happiness is . . .
a smile shared
between friends.

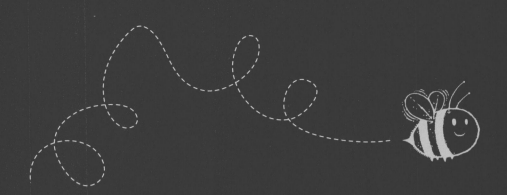

A friend loves at all times.

PROVERBS 17:17

Friends share most everything.
From emotions to wardrobes,
nothing is held back.

The greatest sweetener of
human life is friendship.
JOSEPH ADDISON

Our friends have a way of bringing sunshine, laughter, and joy into our lives.

Friends Forever

Andrea and Amber never knew what it was like to not have each other. Born ten days apart, they were next-door neighbors whose mothers (also best friends) saw their daughters reach every milestone together—from walking and talking to college and marriage....

As young women busy with husbands and careers, Andrea and Amber still made it a priority to spend time together. One afternoon they met for ice cream, and both were surprised when each brought a wrapped gift for the other. They opened them up at the same time to find embroidered baby bibs:

I LOVE MY AUNT ANDREA

I LOVE MY AUNT AMBER

Thus began the next generation of friendship.

A friend is, as it were, a second self.

CICERO

Friendship is where warmth is. . .
where love is. . .where memories thrive.

True friends are experts at
listening and understanding.

A friendship can weather most things and thrive in thin soil; but it needs a little mulch of letters and phone calls and small, silly presents every so often....

PAM BROWN

Understood between girlfriends:

It's perfectly normal to buy a pair of shoes, even if you have absolutely nothing in your closet to wear with them.

Good words to put into practice for a friend:
empathy, helpfulness, warmth, blessing,
thoughtfulness, graciousness, generosity,
kindness, care, consideration.

Friends have all things in common.
PLATO

Girlfriends understand the healing
properties of laughter, chocolate,
and a good, long shopping trip.

Happiness is. . .having a friend
who will skip dessert—
just because you're on a diet.

Wrinkles should merely indicate where smiles have been.

MARK TWAIN

There are few things as important in life as
good friends and shared laughter.

Friends are as companions on a journey
who ought to aid each other to persevere
in the road to a happier life.

PYTHAGORAS

Friendship is a place for comfort,
good hugs, and long talks.

Our friends remind us to laugh. . .to relax. . .
to cherish every moment of every day. . .to enjoy life.

We should give laughter a place in each of our days,
and girlfriends a special place in our hearts.

Laugh and be well.

M. GREEN

If you can eat today, enjoy the sunlight today,
mix good cheer with friends today,
enjoy it and bless God for it.

HENRY WARD BEECHER

A good laugh is sunshine in a house.
WILLIAM MAKEPEACE THACKERAY

Who Knows You Better?

When it comes down to it, who really knows us better than our best friend? As little girls, maybe our moms held that honor, but then came adolescence and that went out the window (at least for a few years). Husbands? That relationship may be the most important one we have on earth, but they still don't always "get" us. Some friends are simply life-stage friends—exactly what we need for a period of time,

but when they move on or we move on, no lasting bond remains. No, a best girlfriend truly is for life. She is the perfect mix of sister, confidante, accountability partner, kindred spirit, and laughter therapist. There truly is no one like her.

I count myself in nothing else so happy as
in a soul remembering my good friends.

WILLIAM SHAKESPEARE

The art of being happy lies in the power of
extracting happiness from common things.

HENRY WARD BEECHER

Happiness is. . .having a friend who shares her last piece of chocolate.

A real friend warms you by her presence,
trusts you with her secrets,
and remembers you in her prayers.

Unknown

Girlfriends and laughter are one of life's greatest combinations—like cake and ice cream, peanut butter and jelly, and popcorn and a movie.

Our mouths were filled with laughter,
our tongues with songs of joy.
PSALM 126:2

Among those whom I like or admire, I can find no common denominator, but among those whom I love, I can: all of them make me laugh.

W. H. Auden

A guaranteed cure for a blue day? . . .
A smile from a friend.

We occasionally have moments when we're perfectly content to feel gloomy. We may even convince ourselves that we somehow "deserve" to feel that way. . . . Then along comes a friend who manages to encourage a smile, and if she tries really hard, can even send you into a fit of laughter.

ANITA WEIGAND

When we count our blessings,
we should count our friends twice—
and those who make us laugh, twice more!

Our friends are ongoing expressions
of heaven's joy!

Without friends no one would choose to live,
though he had all other goods.

ARISTOTLE

Friendship: A place where grace
and understanding abide.

Walk beside me, and just be my friend.
ALBERT CAMUS

The road to a friend's house is never long.

DANISH PROVERB

Two things that make you feel rich:
faithful friends and dark-chocolate truffles.

To have a good friend is one of the highest
delights of life; to be a good friend is
one of the noblest undertakings.

Unknown

No matter what kind of disaster takes place—a bad dye job from the salon, a rip in a pair of jeans while in public, a spilled drink at the lunch table—*girlfriends* find ways to turn the seemingly serious into the most humorous situations ever.

Inside Jokes and Secret Languages

What is it about good friendship that makes everything so easy, so comfortable, so *home*? It doesn't hurt that best friends undoubtedly have their own way of speaking to each other—a wonderful mix of understanding, of shared experiences, of inside jokes, of affection. . . .

It's almost a secret language that nobody else could understand no matter how hard they tried. We know where the other is coming from, and no matter how ridiculous or silly or dysfunctional we may be, we love and accept each other. It's something special just between friends.

A friend who has a joyful spirit brings to earth a smile from God.

It's the love and unwavering loyalty of our friends
that make us feel we've been blessed far more
extravagantly than we deserve.

Friends share laughter,
tears, dreams, disappointments,
and everything in between.

Understood between girlfriends:

Sometimes a girl just needs to cry.

There is nothing on this earth more
to be prized than true friendship.

SAINT THOMAS AQUINAS

A friend is a present you give to yourself.
ROBERT LOUIS STEVENSON

Friendship, like coffee, should be strong with lots of good stuff added in—chocolate included!

A little of what you fancy does you good.
MARIE LLOYD

*Happiness is. . .a much-needed lunch
out with your best friend.*

The happiest days are spent appreciating the simplest joys with your girlfriends.

Friendship is a place where our
hearts always feel at home.

There are many things in life that will catch your eye, but only a few will catch your heart—pursue those.

MICHAEL NOLAN

A few things to cherish: a trusted girlfriend,
a good book, and a secret stash of chocolate.

Love is best of all. There is not, nor ever shall there be, true friendship without it.

Unknown

Time with girlfriends = HAPPY TIME!

A happy heart makes the face cheerful.
PROVERBS 15:13

Girlfriends just know...
A girl can't have too many shades of lipstick,
too many pairs of shoes, or too many girlfriends
to help her decide which ones to buy.

The best indulgences ever:
Overindulging in kindnesses
toward our girlfriends.

Dynamic Duos!

Lucy and Ethel. Wilma and Betty. Laverne and Shirley.
Friends through thick and thin—and a whole lot of
laughs! As you think through the funny memories
you have with your best friends, what sticks out in
your mind? Maybe you fondly remember the lovely
exhaustion you felt after a night of laughter (or the
sore ab muscles you had the next day)!

Perhaps you have an even better time recalling and reliving those memories over and over again. No matter how we found the peanut butter to our jelly, the spaghetti to our meatball, our best friends are truly a gift from God.

Happiness is less indulgent than
it is mandatory—and girlfriends are
a sure way to a lot of happy moments.

When a girlfriend lets you know you have a chocolate smudge on your face, you've been blessed with two pleasures—her company and some really good chocolate!

The hearts of friends are never so quickly
joined as when they laugh together.

Happiness is. . .
laughing about nothing at all
with a special friend.

Girlfriends just know...
Laugh now; laugh later.

A little time for laughter,
A little time to sing,
A little time to be with friends
Will cure most anything.

Verily, great grace may go with a little gift;

And precious are all things that come from friends.

THEOCRITUS

Understood between girlfriends:

It makes perfect sense to buy something you don't
need just because it's on sale.

Even though friends may be separated by miles. . .
even though they may go for months without having
a real conversation. . .they can always pick up right
where they left off. This is true friendship.

Friends open their hearts without hesitation,
speak their thoughts without reservation.

In the presence of a good friend,
even silence is comforting.

The sweetest conversation between friends
is the silent communication of their hearts.

¼ cup of fun

¼ cup of love

¼ cup of compassion

+ ¼ cup of understanding
_____

a girlfriend's heart!

God gives the blessings of friendship and laughter; they're both good for the soul!

A real friend will tell you if you have lipstick on your teeth. . .and then compliment you on the color.

Shopping. Chocolate. Friends.
Thank heaven for life's sweet diversions.

Friends just know...
When you're not sure what to say,
a hug is a great place to start.

Friendship is essentially a partnership.
ARISTOTLE

Friends Are a Blessing

Father, thank You for the blessing of my best friendships. It's amazing to think there was a time when these women weren't a part of my life. But I am glad that time is over and I can proudly claim them as soul sisters. Guard our relationships and make them strong, pure of heart, and always uplifting and encouraging. Our deepest desire is to make You the center of our friendships.

Perfume and incense bring joy to the heart,
and the pleasantness of a friend springs
from their heartfelt advice.

PROVERBS 27:9

The ties of friendship are strengthened by adversity and joy. . .tears and laughter. . . two spoons and one hot fudge sundae.

My best friend is the one who brings out the best in me.

HENRY FORD

Ah, how good it feels. . .the hand of an old friend.
HENRY WADSWORTH LONGFELLOW

Friends touch our lives in ways that no one else can.
They leave lasting imprints on our hearts.

A smile is never an ending,
but always a beautiful beginning.